Holiday Magic Books

*New Year's*

# MAGIC

by James W. Baker
pictures by George Overlie

Lerner Publications Company  Minneapolis

*To my late mother, Hazel Webb Baker, for all her patient
endurance and support over the years as I resolved not to bore
her with yet another magic trick, but always seemed to break
that resolution.*

Library of Congress Cataloging-in-Publication Data

Baker, James W., 1926-
  New Year's magic.

  (Holiday magic books)
  Summary: Describes how to perform magic tricks
with the New Year as a theme.
  1. Tricks—Juvenile literature. 2. New Year—Juvenile literature.
[1. Magic tricks. 2. New Year] I. Overlie, George, ill. II. Title.
III. Series: Baker, James W., 1926-   . Holiday magic books.
GV1548.B343  1989                    793.8                    88-24449
ISBN 0-8225-2231-4 (lib. bdg.)

Manufactured in the United States of America

1   2   3   4   5   6   7   8   9   10   98   97   96   95   94   93   92   91   90   89

# CONTENTS

# INTRODUCTION

With noisemakers, balloons, and confetti, with lanterns, fireworks, and giant paper dragons, and with prayers, people all over the world welcome the new year. In the United States and Japan, the new year is celebrated on January 1st, but in Vietnam and China, the exact date changes from year to year. In some other countries, people celebrate the new year for a few days in the spring.

The new year is a time to part with the past and prepare for the future. Some people clean their houses or eat certain foods so they will have good luck, health, and wealth in the next year. Others make resolutions to correct faults and bad habits in hopes of making the next year better than before.

However you celebrate the new year, resolve to learn and perform the magic tricks in this book. Entertain your friends and family as you welcome a "magical" new year.

# HAPPY NEW YEAR

## HOW IT LOOKS

Have a volunteer from the audience pick a card and then return it to the middle of the deck. You shuffle the cards. Have the volunteer deal cards onto the table, spelling "Happy New Year" one card at a time. When she completes the spelling, the final card will be her chosen card.

## HOW TO MAKE IT

For this trick, you will need a deck of cards. Depending on the size of your hands, you should use bridge size cards or miniature cards.

1. You fan the deck of cards facedown and have a volunteer pick a card. Then you square up the deck and cut it near the center.

2. Have the volunteer place her card on top of the pile in your left hand. Hold the pile in the palm of your hand with your fingers curled around it (**Figure 1**).

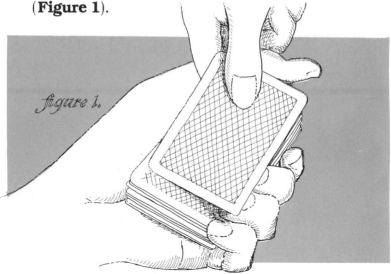

figure 1.

**3.** Place the pile in your right hand on top of the pile in your left. Hold the tip of your left little finger between the two piles (**Figure 2**). Riffle the outer ends of the cards a few times but keep looking right in the eyes of the volunteer. Do not look at your hands.

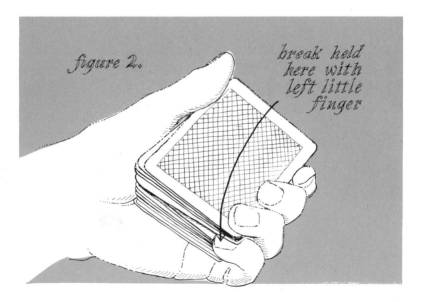

figure 2.

break held here with left little finger

**4.** Grasp the cards with your right fingers at the front, thumb at the back, and cut the cards at the break held by your little finger so that all of the cards below the break stay in your left hand. Shuffle the cards, making sure the top card in your left hand falls last, so it remains on top. The selected card is now on the top of the deck.

**5.** Deal one card facedown on the table for each letter in "Happy New Year." The first card dealt will be the selected card. As you deal it facedown on the table say "H." Deal the second card on top of the first and say "A." Deal the third card and say "P," and so on until you've spelled "Happy New Year."

**6.** When you've finished spelling "Happy New Year" by dealing the last card and saying "R," stop dealing and turn over that last card. It is *not* the selected card and it looks like you have failed. Pretend to be embarrassed and say that you forgot to tap the deck.

**7.** Take the cards from the table and put them on top of the deck. The chosen card was on the bottom of the pile on the table and is buried in the deck when the cards are replaced.

**8.** Tap the top of the deck and hand it to the volunteer. Ask her to spell "Happy New Year" just as you did, dealing one card for each letter.

**9.** When she finishes, ask her to turn over the last card dealt. It will be the card she originally selected.

# A RING'S PREDICTIONS

## HOW IT LOOKS

You borrow a finger ring and drop it onto a pencil. As your friend asks questions about her fortune in the New Year, the ring mysteriously rises halfway up the pencil for "Yes" and all the way up for "No" to answer her questions.

1. Tie a thin black thread to an unsharpened pencil where the metal piece meets the pencil wood.
2. Tie the other end of the black thread to the lowest button on your shirt. Be sure you are wearing a dark-colored shirt so your audience will not see the thread.
3. Put the pencil in your shirt pocket.

1. Take the pencil out of your pocket and hold it with the eraser pointing up. Borrow a finger ring from a member of the audience and drop the ring over the end of the pencil and the thread. Be sure you have enough slack in the thread so that the ring will drop to the bottom of the pencil and rest on your hand (**Figure 1**).

**2.** By moving the pencil slowly away from your body, you can make the ring rise up the pencil. You can stop the ring halfway up the pencil or, by moving your hand a little farther, make the ring rise nearly to the top (**Figure 2**). To make the ring go down, simply move your hand slowly toward your body.

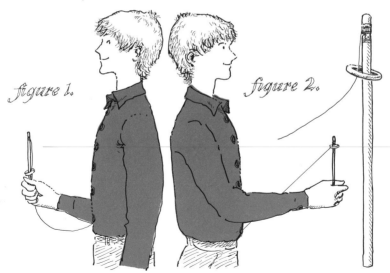

*figure 1.*

*figure 2.*

**3.** Have your friend ask "yes or no" questions about her fortune in the New Year. You decide which answer to give and make the ring rise halfway up the pencil for "Yes" and all the way up for "No" to answer each question.

**4.** When you've finished answering questions, turn the pencil upside down and let the ring drop off in your hand. Hand the ring back to the person you borrowed it from and place the pencil back in your pocket.

Note: This trick can be very baffling and very funny—depending on the questions asked and the answers given—but the conditions must be right. You should perform in a slightly darkened room at some distance from your audience and you must wear dark clothing so the black thread cannot be seen.

# A NEW YEAR PENNY

## HOW IT LOOKS

Tell your friend something like "I am going to make a New Year penny, that is, a penny of the current year, go through this table. Only a New Year penny will work," you say, "because it is the only penny that can soften the surface of a table." Place the penny on the table and set a salt shaker on it. Cover the salt shaker with a paper napkin and the salt shaker—not the penny—goes through the table.

## HOW TO MAKE IT

For this trick, you will need a penny of the current year, a salt shaker, and a paper napkin. You will also need to sit at a table across from your friend.

*figure 1.*

1. Place a New Year penny on the table and set a salt shaker on top of it. Form a paper napkin around the salt shaker so that the napkin takes on the shape of the shaker (**Figure 1**).

2. Pick up the shaker with the napkin around it and tell your friend to note whether the penny is heads-up or tails-up. As you do this, draw the napkin-covered salt shaker back toward you.

3. Cover the penny again with the salt shaker. Tell your friend you'll give him another look at the penny before you make it go through the table.

4. Once again, pick up the shaker with the napkin around it, drawing it back towards you.

18

**5.** When the napkin-covered shaker just clears the edge of the table, loosen your grip on the napkin very slightly and let the salt shaker drop silently in your lap. Be sure to hold your legs together so the shaker doesn't fall all the way to the floor.

**6.** Place the paper napkin—which still looks like it holds the shaker—over the penny again. Your friend will assume the shaker is inside the napkin.

**7.** Holding the paper napkin with one hand, raise your other hand above and suddenly bring it down on the paper napkin, crushing it flat on the table.

**8.** Pick up the crushed napkin and apologize because the penny is still on the table. Tell your friend the penny must have softened the table so that the salt shaker went through the table instead. Reach into your lap, get the shaker, and place it back on top of the table.

# CHINESE NEW YEAR

## HOW IT LOOKS

Show the audience a strip of paper with Chinese characters written on it. Explain that it says Happy New Year in Chinese. Talk about how the Chinese enjoy the New Year's celebration so much that even if this Happy New Year sign is destroyed, it will be magically restored. Tear up the paper into small pieces. You say the magic words "Gung Hay Fat Choy"—Happy New Year in Chinese. Immediately the paper is restored to its original condition.

1. Cut out two pieces of yellow construction paper, each about 1 inch (2.5 cm) by 10 inches (25 cm).

2. Mark each piece with the characters for Gung Hay Fat Choy as shown (**Figure 1**) so that the two pieces look exactly alike.

figure 1.

3. Fold one of the strips like an accordion and paste it to the end of the other strip. The characters should face *out* on both strips (**Figure 2**).

figure 2.

1. Show both sides of the unfolded paper to the audience, covering the pasted-on accordion with your left hand.

2. Tear the unfolded paper into several pieces by ripping the width of the paper (**Figure 3**). Put the scraps in front of the accordion in your left hand.

figure 3.

3. When you have torn the entire strip of paper, crumple the pieces and the accordion together in your right palm.

4. Say "Gung Hay Fat Choy," and with the torn pieces hidden in your right hand, slowly draw the accordion out with your left hand. Keep the tension tight so the folds can't be seen.

## CALENDAR MIND READING

*HOW IT LOOKS*

Randomly arranged on the floor are 12 pages (months) from a calendar. While you are out of the room, a volunteer from the audience touches one of the months. When you come back into the room, your assistant touches various months, asking you "Is it this one?" Since you can read your assistant's mind, you say "No" until your assistant touches the correct one. Then you say "Yes."

## HOW TO MAKE IT

For this trick, you will need a calendar that has 12 pages, one for each month. Separate the pages so you have 12 sheets of paper with one month on each. You will also need an assistant.

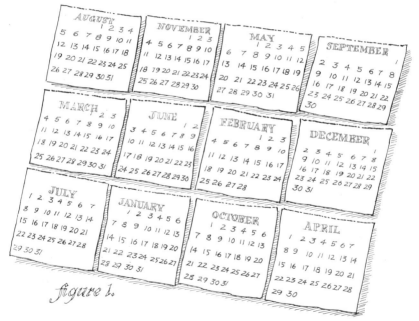

figure 1.

## HOW TO DO IT

**1.** Arrange the 12 calendar months on the floor (**Figure 1**) in any random order.

**2.** Leave the room and have a volunteer from the audience touch one of the months.

**3.** When you return to the room, your assistant lets you know which was the chosen month by signaling on the *very first month* she touches. She does this by touching any other month in the spot which corresponds to the position of the chosen month in the pattern of pages (**Figure 2**).

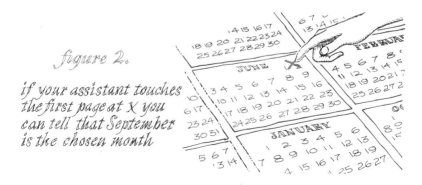

*figure 2.*

*if your assistant touches the first page at X you can tell that September is the chosen month*

**4.** Do the trick several times, leaving the room each time, returning, and correctly saying "Yes" when your assistant finally touches the selected month.

**5.** Then do the trick one final time, but this time, allow your assistant to touch only the first page. (This, of course, tells you which month has been selected.)

**6.** Stop your assistant and tell the audience that to prove there is no signaling you will let anyone in the audience point to various months. Still you choose the correct month because your assistant signaled it to you when she first touched a month.

## HOW IT LOOKS

Tell your friend that whenever you think of the New Year you are reminded of the seven most important dates of each month. Show seven index cards, each with a different number, saying these are the seven most important dates in any month because they are magic dates. Have your friend secretly select one of the magic dates and write it down on a slip of paper without you seeing.

Lay all seven index cards facedown on the table and begin tapping them one at a time. Have your friend spell his number mentally, letter by letter, as you tap. On the final letter, he says "Stop" and you stop tapping on that card. Turn the card over and on it will be the number your friend selected.

## HOW TO MAKE IT

For this trick, you will need seven index cards with the following numbers written on them: 2, 5, 7, 11, 13, 16, and 17. You will also need a pen and a piece of paper.

**1.** Each number on the index cards is spelled with a different number of letters:

$$2 = \text{T-W-O}$$
$$5 = \text{F-I-V-E}$$
$$7 = \text{S-E-V-E-N}$$
$$11 = \text{E-L-E-V-E-N}$$
$$16 = \text{S-I-X-T-E-E-N}$$
$$13 = \text{T-H-I-R-T-E-E-N}$$
$$17 = \text{S-E-V-E-N-T-E-E-N}$$

Note that "2" has three letters, "5" has four letters, "7" has five letters, "11" has six letters, and so on.

**2.** Show the seven cards and say that they have the seven most important calendar dates on them, the magic dates. Don't say anything about spelling.

**3.** Ask your friend to choose one of the seven dates and write it down on a slip of paper. Have him fold the paper so you can't see the number he chose.

**4.** Next, you place the seven index cards on a table *facedown* in a circle. They *must* be placed in the order shown (**Figure 1**) and you must memorize this order.

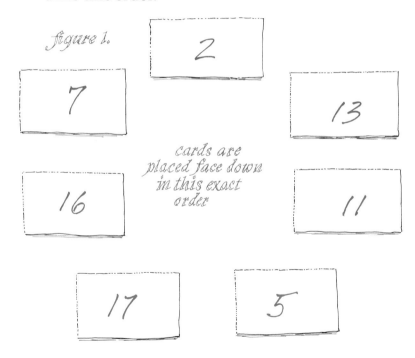

figure 1.

7

2

13

16

cards are placed face down in this exact order

11

17

5

**5.** With a pencil, begin tapping on the cards, apparently in random order, telling your friend to spell his number as you tap, one letter for each tap.

**6.** Make the first two taps on any cards, but on the third tap, hit the "2" so that if your friend is spelling "T-W-O," he will say "Stop" as he completes his spelling and you will turn up his card.

**7.** For the next tap, jump over two cards clockwise to the "5." Next, jump over two more to the "7," then over two more to the "11," and so on around the circle, turning over the correct number when you hear "Stop."

For example, suppose your friend selects "7." He spells silently "S-E-V-E-N" as you tap. On the final letter, "N", he says "Stop" and you stop tapping on that card. Turn the card over and on it will be "7," the number your friend selected.

## HAVE A MAGICAL NEW YEAR

### HOW IT LOOKS

You have your friend try to cut a deck of cards exactly in half. After he does some math, you have him count to a certain card, look at it, and give the deck back to you. You pick up the deck and deal cards from the top, spelling aloud the phrase "H-A-V-E A M-A-G-I-C-A-L N-E-W Y-E-A-R." The last card dealt will be the one your friend looked at.

## HOW TO MAKE IT

For this trick, you will need a deck of 52 cards.

## HOW TO DO IT

**1.** Ask your friend to cut a deck of cards in half, being as exact as possible. Have him choose one of the halves and count the cards in that half. Then have him add the digits together to get his target number.

If he counted 28 cards, he would add 2 + 8 to get 10. If he counted 23, he would add 2 + 3 to get 5.

**2.** Have him count from the *bottom* of his half-deck to his target number. Without showing you, he looks at the card which is at his target number and then places his half-deck on top of the other half.

If his target number was 10, he would look at the tenth card. If it was 3, the third card.

**3.** You pick up the entire deck and deal the cards from the top, spelling aloud the phrase "H-A-V-E A M-A-G-I-C-A-L N-E-W Y-E-A-R," one letter for each card dealt. The last card dealt will be the one your friend looked at.

The procedure described always brings you to the 19th card from the top of the deck. Since the phrase "Have a Magical New Year" has 19 letters you will always end up with the correct card.

You turn your back while your friend selects any month of the calendar and draws a square around nine dates. Your friend tells you the smallest of these nine numbers. You do some math and announce the sum of the nine dates without ever seeing the calendar page.

For this trick, you will need a calendar, a pencil, and a piece of paper.

1. While your back is turned, have your friend select any month of the calendar and draw a square around nine dates.
2. When your friend tells you the smallest of the nine numbers, you add 8 to it and multiply the result by 9. That will give you the sum of the nine numbers.

For example: if the square includes 5, 6, 7, 12, 13, 14, 19, 20, and 21, those nine numbers added together equal 117. To predict that total, you would add the smallest number (5) to 8 and multiply the result by 9.

$$5 + 8 = 13$$
$$13 \times 9 = 117$$

NEW YEAR'S EVE
NOISEMAKERS

## HOW IT LOOKS

Tell a story something like "Three friends had a party to celebrate New Year's Eve. Each had a noisemaker." On a table are three wooden matchboxes, which represent the three noisemakers. You pick up each one and shake it so that the audience can hear matches rattling inside.

"One of the three friends was a magician and at midnight he wiggled his fingers over the three noisemakers." Wiggle your fingers over the matchboxes. Have a volunteer from the audience open the three matchboxes. She discovers that the matches inside have vanished and in their place are three crumpled paper napkins. On one is written "Happy," on another is "New," and on the third one is "Year."

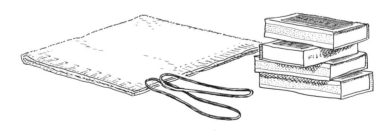

## HOW TO MAKE IT

**1.** For this trick, you will need a plain paper napkin, a felt-tip pen, four boxes of wooden matches, two rubber bands, and a long-sleeve shirt.

**2.** Cut three small squares from the napkin. Write "Happy" on one, "New" on another, and "Year" on the third. Crumple the squares and put one in each of three empty matchboxes.

**3.** Fill the fourth matchbox about half full of wooden matches and attach it to your right wrist with two rubber bands (**Figure 1**). Cover this matchbox with your long sleeve so the audience cannot see it.

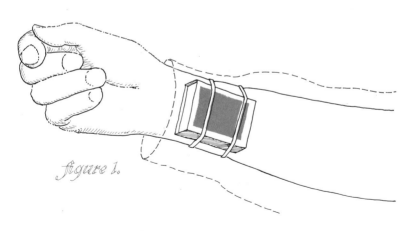

figure 1.

1. With the three matchboxes containing paper napkins on the table, tell the story about the three friends celebrating New Year's Eve together and their noisemakers.

2. Pick up each matchbox from the table with your right hand and shake it. The audience will hear the matches rattling in the box attached to your wrist and assume there are matches in each of the three boxes on the table.

3. When you come to midnight in the story, wiggle the fingers of your left hand over the three boxes on the table, keeping your right hand still so no matches rattle. Ask someone to open the three matchboxes.

4. Watch the expressions on the faces of your audience when they see that the matches have vanished and in their place are pieces of paper saying "Happy New Year."

# HOW QUICKLY THE NEW YEAR PASSES

## HOW IT LOOKS

A volunteer from the audience chooses a card which is then hopelessly lost in the deck as you talk about weeks, months, and years, dealing cards onto the table and placing them back on the deck. Suddenly the chosen card mysteriously appears on the top of the deck.

## HOW TO MAKE IT

For this trick, you will need a deck of cards with the bottom card reversed, or faceup, while all the other cards are facedown.

**1.** Fan the cards *facedown* without showing the reversed card on the bottom of the deck. Have a volunteer choose a card and, without showing you what it is, show it to the audience.

**2.** Cut the deck at the point where the chosen card is taken. Hold the top half in your right hand and the bottom half, with the reversed card on the bottom, in your left hand (**Figure 1**).

*figure 1.*

*reversed card on bottom*

**3.** Have the volunteer put the chosen card on top of the pack in your right hand. Drop the pack in your left hand on top and tell the volunteer her card is lost in the pack.

43

**4.** Spread the cards out *faceup* and pretend to look for the chosen card. Act surprised when you come to the reversed card but don't reveal the chosen card above it (**Figure 2**).

**5.** Take all the cards below the reversed card and place them *faceup* on top (**Figure 3**). Then turn the entire deck over. Now the reversed card will be faceup on top of the deck (**Figure 4**). Turn it over so all cards are *facing down*.

figure 2.

figure 3.

figure 4.

**6.** Ask the volunteer how many weeks there are in a year. When she says "52," deal a pile of five cards onto the table, one at a time, and then a pile of two cards. Pick up the two cards, put them on top of the five cards, and place all seven back on top of the deck.

**7.** Ask the volunteer how many months there are in a year. When she says "12," deal 12 cards onto the table. Pick them up and put them back on top of the deck.

**8.** Ask the volunteer how many days there are in a week. When she says "7," deal seven cards onto the table. Pick them up and put them on top of the deck.

**9.** Put the deck on the table and ask the volunteer what time it is. Without waiting for an answer, tell her you think it is time to find her card. Ask her what her card was. When she answers, turn the top card on the deck over. It will be the card she chose.

# TRICKS FOR BETTER MAGIC

Here are some simple rules you should keep in mind while learning to perform the tricks in this book.

1. Read the entire trick several times until you thoroughly understand it.
2. Practice the trick alone or in front of a mirror until you feel comfortable doing the trick, then present it to an audience.
3. Learn to perform one trick perfectly before moving on to another trick. It is better to perform one trick well than a half dozen poorly.
4. Work on your "presentation." Make up special "patter" (what you say while doing a trick) that is funny and entertaining. Even the simplest trick becomes magical when it is properly presented.
5. Choose tricks that suit you and your personality. Some tricks will work better for you than others.

Stick with these. *Every* trick is not meant to be performed by *every* magician.

6. Feel free to experiment and change a trick to suit you and your unique personality so that you are more comfortable presenting it.

7. Never reveal the secret of the trick. Your audience will respect you much more if you do not explain the trick. When asked how you did a trick, simply say "by magic."

8. Never repeat a trick for the same audience. If you do, you will have lost the element of surprise and your audience will probably figure out how you did it the second time around.

9. Take your magic seriously, but not yourself. Have fun with magic and your audience will have fun along with you.

## ABOUT THE AUTHOR

James W. Baker, a magician for over 30 years, has performed as "Mister Mystic" in hospitals, orphanages, and schools around the world. He is a member of the International Brotherhood of Magicians and the Society of American Magicians, and is author of *Illusions Illustrated*, a magic book for young performers.

From 1951 to 1963, Baker was a reporter for *The Richmond (VA) News Leader*. From 1963 to 1983, he was an editor with the U.S. Information Agency, living in Washington, D.C., India, Turkey, Pakistan, the Philippines, and Tunisia, and traveling in 50 other countries. Today Baker and his wife, Elaine, live in Williamsburg, Virginia, where he performs magic and writes for the local newspaper, *The Virginia Gazette*.

## ABOUT THE ARTIST

George Overlie is a talented artist who has illustrated numerous books. Born in the small town of Rose Creek, Minnesota, Overlie graduated from the New York Phoenix School of Design and began his career as a layout artist. He soon turned to book illustration and proved his skill and versatility in this demanding field. For Overlie, fantasy, illusion, and magic are all facets of illustration and have made doing the Holiday Magic books a real delight.